Always More French Fries at the Bottom of the Bag

--a collection of poems and spiritual reflections.

John D. Emens

Copyright 2019 John D. Emens
All rights reserved.
ISBN:978-1-7323147-1-9

Dedicated to friends in adversity

A friend loves at all times and a brother is born for adversity. (Proverbs 17:17)

Friends indeed

Michael L. Schurch &
Rush Creek Press in production assistance prayer

Introduction

*In many ways, this book is a follow-on to my previous work, **"Boom! & Adversity"** (2018). These poems and reflections are illuminations of a thankfully broken man. Recently having my right leg amputated due to a fall and ensuing infection, and having my kidneys fail with now dialysis, I am definitely suffering grievous injury. Yet, through my ordeal and adversity I have grown in mind and spirit and am far better for it. I have found that peace and joy are not based on circumstances, but rather come from the spirit and the soul. This being so, equipped with the joy of salvation in my heart and soul, I have managed to be quite content despite the deleterious difficulties I have experienced in the past three years; this includes ten major surgeries to try and save my leg. True, disappointments have been severe at times, but I still rejoice in what the Maker has done for me. This will never change, and for this I am eternally grateful.*

There is so much beauty in the world, despite its woe and cause for worry. Let us be thankful, and move to a place where love, peace, & hope prevail.

Blessings,

J.D. Emens
Marion, Ohio
February 2019

Contents

Always More French Fries at the bottom of the Bag 1

People are like Bugs 3

Permission Slip 4

Thinking of the Upside 6

Even If 8

Empty Nest 10

Uniforms 11

Shadow-boxing at Noon 12

We Don't Hear the Cries 13

Broken Typewriter 14

Everyday Child 15

Addiction 16

The Dance 17

God's Wrath 18

The Machine. 19

The Hound 20

For the Children 21

Running Sore 22

Hating God 23

Young Love 24

Sugar Daddy 25

Eye of the Needle 26

The Girl Next Door 27

Fear 28

Cattitude	30
In the Beginning	32
Small piece of Heaven	34
Shame	35
They Choose Us	37
Best Soldiers	38
Conditional Love	40
Public Bath	42
No Panic In Heaven	43
Unwanted Return	44
Mon Amie—a Tribute	45
Pain	46
Holidays	47
The Myth	48
Life Preserver	49
The Rattler	51
The MRS	52
People like Trees	53
Sullen Sunbeam	54
Lonely Scarecrow	56
Why Weeping?	57
Dry Season	58
Propitiation	59
Asbestos Land	60
God's People	61
Backpack Blues	62

Photo Album 64

Alabaster Blanket 66

Silly Lilly 67

Bad Reaction 68

My Popper 70

Ice Trays 72

Poopydoo 74

"Joekeeze!" 77

Big C 78

Lost Doves 80

Epilogue 82

About the Book and its Author 84

Always More French Fries at the bottom of the Bag

Life is like a bag of French fries from a drive-thru burger joint. Gobbling hot, greasy, salty, tasty 'taters temporally sates all the world's problems with belly driven dopamine to the brain. As we glibly stuff fries in our mouths and guzzle ice cold *Mountain Dew*, all is made right in the moment.

But then the food runs out, just like in life good times can turn south at moments least expected. Job loss. Sickness. Divorce. Kids discover opioids. Parents die. Bankruptcy, Identity Theft. Gown frocked pulpit people touching what they shouldn't.

--all these tough seasons come upon us like fire on dry brush in a wicked windstorm of misery.

We don't understand. We always went to church. We tithed. Were faithful in the Word. We followed the golden rule.

So when it all hits the fan, we look heavenward and shake our fist. We reconsider and begin to bargain with our Maker. We make promises to be better in the hopes the copasetic times will return. We may pray our rear ends off and shed tears unending.

Sometimes things turn around; sometimes not. When they don't, we have a choice: egregious anger toward the sky, or accept His will and seek a silver lining. Understand we may never understand, and through resignation of control we have peace.

And as we move through our failures or dead-end tragedies, we glom onto the knowledge that we've grown closer to Him. We are made whole through suffering, and the scars we bear make us stronger, more compassionate, and perhaps, yes, more faithful and obedient.

Through tough seasons we have the chance to love Him despite calamity, and in doing so we become more like Him, who loves us without fail despite our worst waywardness. Unconditional love is tough, but He does it for us; likewise, *we should do it for Him.*

When the fire is out, and the light seeps in at daybreak, we realize the bag of the French fries of life was never really empty. No, there always more fries at the bottom of the bag when through the ordeal we learn and grow closer to our Maker.

In the end, we smile, and now illuminated, we realize maybe that growing closer to Him was the divine purpose of the whole struggle in the first place.

Yes, God does practice tough love too.

Amen.

People are like Bugs

People are like bugs. Some small, cute and fuzzy. Others big and scary. Most harmless. Some deadly. The trick is sussing out the good vs. the bad bugs. Looks can be deceiving. Yellow Jacket bumblebees hum sweet, and are colorful, yet have a mighty sting. Others are more obvious, like the intrepid black wasps whom can levy harm at any time. Likewise, the fetching lass may be sweet but only digging gold, and the shiny cop may hold a powerful badge for the wrong reasons.

Like a drug pusher, some bugs are deadly poisonous; other bugs are innocuous, harmless as a monarch butterfly. Some bugs eat other bugs, which may be a good thing. Some have pleasant raison d'etre, like pollinating or making sweet honey. Other, like termites, seem to serve little purpose.

In the end though, we realize there is some good bug and bad bug in all of us. We champion our strong suits yet still harbor flaws. But like the moth or butterfly, we can start one way, and end up another.

Yes, some bugs may morph or change over time, whilst others stay true to themselves and others. Some get squashed and some smoosh others. Some people are like the ladybug bringing good fortune to others.

In the end, bugs are just bugs like people are just people. We all are teeny weenie organisms on the ant hill of life. Living by instincts and surviving just to spawn and eventually pass on. When we cease to exist---no longer able to bug anyone at all—our goodness and badness is revealed, and we end up in a place of our own doings.

And gnat is the all there is to know

Permission Slip

They sat on her sofa and watched the New Year's ball drop in Times Square. "Man, I can't believe it is 2020!" she uttered as she sipped her champagne. "I know," said the man as he scooched closer and placed his arm around her. "Paul, I really had a good time tonight," she cooed with a randy smile. "Yeah, me too."

He looked into her hazel eyes and said, "Rachel, I would really like to kiss you." "Sounds good to me." "Small problem, I didn't bring my permission slips with me tonight." She laughed, and said, "No worries, we don't need to put it in writing; you have my consent." "No way. I can't kiss or touch you unless you sign off on it—you know that. Later you could come back and call it sexual harassment."

"Paul, I would never do that!" "Well, I am not going to kiss you without you signing for it." "Well, here is a piece of paper. I will write it out that—is that okay?" "Please, Rachel, also write that you are not under the influence—that could nullify the disclaimer." "But I had some champagne, Paul"

Paul sighed, and said, "I can't kiss you tonight then, Sorry." "Don't you trust me?" "Yes. But you know what Samuel Clemens aptly said, *'Trust everyone but always cut the cards.'*" "You are being silly." "Can't do it. Rach, I think I better go. We got that board meeting in the morning." "Can I at least have a hug good night?" "Sorry. No official permission slip; no hugs."

"Okay. I understand. Maybe we could get together tomorrow night?" "Good idea. Let's finalize plans tomorrow." "Will you at least shake my hand?" she uttered with a wan smile. "Sure."

(They carefully shook hands).

Paul got up to leave. As he shut the door behind him, he confided, "You know, I really wanted to do more than kiss you tonight—I really like you." "Me too," she said dourly. "Gotta go."

Before he shut the door behind him, he groused under his breath, *"God I hate 21st century dating."* "Me too," She replied. "Good night Rachael." "G'night."

(The door was shut).

Welcome to the modern world; two beating hearts separated by a piece of paper

Thinking of the Upside

Trudging home from school, Colin turned to Noah and said, "What's wrong man? You seem kinda down." "Nuthin'" "Don't give me that. You can't even look me in the eye." "Well, my mom and dad are going to call it quits; dad moved out last weekend."

(Noah hung his head).

Colin bit his lip. Smacking Noah on the back he chirped, "Well, think of the upside." "The upside?" "Yeah. Noah, you know that new iPhone you wanted?"

(Noah nodded).

"Well, ask your dad for it. Then ask your mom for a new skateboard you told me you wanted." "Colin, that won't help the situation" "Oh. Forget that. Just get stuff, man." "Colin—why would they?" "Man, they did you wrong. Time to cash in. Heck, Blake's parents split up and he got a brand-new off-road bike and a new catcher's mitt out of it."

(Noah brightened).

"Huh. What I really want is a new **PlayStation II**." "Well Noah, just mope a bit, or act kinda disturbed. You'll get your video player, and more, if you play your cards right." "Okay Colin, what if they don't' give in?" "Then start wiggin' out and stuff. And ask separately. Once your dad coughs up sompin', your mom will have to do the same---trust me, it works every time."

Noah nodded, and then with a broad smile said, "Man—this could be better than Christmas!" "Now you're thinkin' dude." "Man, Colin, I never looked at it this way" "Dude, you're golden. My parents are starting to fight a lot now. I'm kinda hoping things don't work out 'cause I want that **Black Panther** pinball machine."

"Cool!" "Remember one thing, Noah. Don't act like, well, sort of well-adjusted to everything. Then you won't get diddly." "Okay Colin but what if they don't bite? Ya know, get me the stuff." "Well, Noah—mess things up." "Whaddya mean?"

(Colin shrugged).

"You know—get bad grades or start taking money from their purses and stuff. Works every time." "Colin?" "Yeah?" "Thanks for being such a good bud. Man, this could be so great." "And it's only the beginning" "What do you mean?" "In a couple years you will be driving. Maybe there is a set of wheels in it for you down the line." "You think so?" "I know so. Blake's older brother just got a bitchin' new truck." "This is soo great!"

(A pause).

"Noah, you want to go to the arcade?" "Nahh. Got no money, Colin." "Well, let's go to your place and '*find*' some money, if you know what I mean." "Great idea. I know where mom keeps a stash in her bedroom."

(Colin nodded and grinned).

"What if we get caught? You know, she spots the mullah gone?" "That's what we want!"

(A broad smile flickered across Noah's face).

"I get it."

A moment later, Noah stopped walking. He exclaimed, "You know, this could be the best thing that *ever* happened to me!" "Now you're talkin' Noah!"

The sun now was out, and there was a light, soothing breeze. A broad grin creased Noah's face as he pondered all the possibilities. As he walked, there was a new skip in his step.

He smiled the whole way home

Even If

With an infected leg I prayed fervently for healing. Ten surgeries from the best surgeons ensued. Almost three years of prayer and supplication for the leg to be cured. To no avail. And, after multiple rounds of massively strong antibiotics to save the leg, the kidneys weakened more and more. I had many churches in the area, as well as my, family, and friends praying for a miraculous intervention by Lord. Yet, I still lost the leg, and the kidneys still failed. I am now on dialysis.

Was God listening? Did He hear my prayers? Yes. Absolutely. And for whatever reason, He simply replied, "No." Full stop.

Am I a bad person? *Is God angry with me?* Do I deserve these maladies for previous misdeeds on my part? This I do not know.

I do know that through this ordeal He brought me to the *"even if"* place, where I understood the preeminence of His providential will. I ended up praying for healing, but acknowledged that *even if* He didn't heal me, I would be willing to accept His will, lock, stock, and barrel.

Thankfully, in His own way, He delivered me. In truth I didn't get what I wanted. He didn't cure me, but He continued to give me peace and joy. And for this I am grateful.

There is a difference between healing and curing. I wasn't cured. I lost my leg, and my kidneys failed. Yet through my ordeal, I have been actualized, realized, understood, and felt the deep love from Above. My soul has been made more whole, healthy, and yes, even happy. My heart is broken for my physical misfortune, but like in any tragedy, big or small, time has eased my pain.

The Lord promises in the **Book of Joel** that He will *"replace what the locusts have taken."* Will He like in the **Book of Job** twice restore my fortunes? Probably not. But He has given me so much more, namely, more of knowledge of Him and His ways and His person. Actually, the suffering has endeared me more to Him.

In **Psalm 119** it reads, *"It is a good for me that I have been afflicted, so that I might learn Your statutes."* This is tough, but scathingly true. Regardless of the pain and suffering, I am better for the ouch. Nobody likes to be stretched, let alone put through the mill, yet, spiritual enlargement does not always come at a time of our choosing. Difficult seasons do reap bountiful crops of personal growth.

I won't ever walk right, nor perhaps ever work or practice the trade of my avocation again, but I can submit, be thankful, and fulfill my new calling of His choice. Do I know exactly as to where I am being led? No. But when orders are changed from Above, I have little to say, but to acquiesce, and thankfully accept the new role provided.

Life isn't always about first choices. It is about His choices. When His choices become my choices, I know I am more what I ought to be—and it feels wonderful. It may not be easy, but there is tremendous satisfaction in truly being useful.

I am a broken man Yet, like any mending bone--even though once broken--with time I am stronger after the reconstruction. Scars fade, but wisdom and illumination are reaped. Learning does come at a price.

In the end I have had to accept the *"even if,"* yet I still so gratefully and thankfully live on

Empty Nest

When the mother wren tosses her young out of the nest, for them, it is a shock. They now have to fly to survive. Life tosses us all out of our little nests, our comfort zones. Sometimes we see change coming; other times we are blindsided.

Term it as you will. Perhaps a "growing experience," or being "stretched." When life pushes us, we tend to balk, blister, or boo hoo. But unless we face our obstacles head on, we sometimes miss the point.

At times, *God puts us in positions we cannot control so He can be in control.* When curve balls come our way, we grow closer to Him, and rely on our Maker to guide us. Through travail, we learn about ourselves, but also about Him. Although in the heat of battle we may feel alone, in the end we can look back and see His intricate care the whole entire way.

These challenges teach us to trust the One and Only. Pray not the difficulty go away. Rather, pray He helps us see through the rough & tumble. We may not always get the outcome we desire, but we glean His character through the struggle. We get to not just believe in Him, but to truly know Him. Just as importantly, we can learn to become more like Him,

So when life goes south, come against the folly of a "Why me?" attitude, and look to heavens and say, "Thank you!" For everyone knows the best metals are forged in fire.

We are the same.

Amen.

Uniforms

We all wear uniforms, be in sports, job, or war. We use them to identify and separate the good guys from the bad. The better from the worse. Truth be known, uniforms and accoutrements are only skin deep. They tell us what is on the outside.

We have to see beyond the badge or briefcase and look to the heart and soul. None of us is completely good or bad. We all make mistakes, and yet we all can bless. It is what the uniforms represent that misconstrue. When the cop shoots in the wrong, or the priest touches what he shouldn't, we are appalled.

We always need to evaluate the person—not the outer garb—what the shroud of the uniform projects. We know full well that the grungy homeless chap may be a saint diamond in the rough, or a well-dressed bloke might actually be a pauper. These blithe observations just show that simple profiling is too easy and frequently wrong. Stereotypes are shortcuts, and soundbites always make sense.

But all of us—like life itself, are complex and our situations unique. And by judging too quickly we misconstrue or miss the mark. We need to stop appraising by appearances and have the courage to look a cut deeper. Humanity is a right—not bubble-gum wrapper. And the true test isn't in the empirical—the car, the house, or the bank account, but in the intangibles, such as love, compassion, generosity, and truth.

Virtue is like fruit. The good stuff is below the skin, and how we clothe ourselves isn't nearly as important as how we act toward others. Eternal crowns are a reward for caring; not a symbol of attainment or rule.

So put the uniforms aside and start washing dirty feet. For in the end, we all could use a good bath, regardless of whether we slumber in satin sheets or a roadside sleeping bag.

Selah (Pause and calmly think of that!)

Shadow-boxing at Noon

"Truth is truth."

"Skin is only beauty deep."

"What comes around goes around."

"Root is the money of all evil."

"Small things come in big packages."

"The more the same, the more things seem to change."

"The soul is the mirror of the eyes."

"All reasons happen for a thing."

"If God is against us, who can be for us?"

More than anything else is the old yarn about the scared, foolish wolf who cried,

"BOY!"

We Don't Hear the Cries

The recession is over, let us strike up the band. Rough times are over. The recovery is at hand. No more hunger. No more pain. No more worry. No more blame. Unemployment is down, and business is up. Let's go shop, 'cause we just need the stuff.

So who kept their jobs? For whom did the bell toll? No, we don't hear the cries of those who fell off the rolls.

Amen.

Broken Typewriter

(Missed a period)

She wrapped her arms around him with spritely glee thinking," Tonight is the night!" He fumbled with the condom putting it on. When they began, the protection came off. But he didn't care. No bones about it, he knew the rubber came off.

He was close. So he spilled his seed.

She never knew the condom came off—at least not right away. He dropped her like a hot potato when the seed took hold. He rationalized, *"I mean, Jesus! It wasn't my fault she was too loose! Besides, it was an away game.*

Everyday Child

Tanya drove her lightning blue late model ***Lincoln Navigator*** through a white neighborhood. Felicia was in the front seat playing a video game. They came to a stop light. Tanya waited. Felicia was too wrapped up in her game to care.

The light changed. Tanya stepped on the gas. They came to a new intersection. There was tanning salon on the corner. White people were going in and out.

Felicia looked up and asked, "Mom, why do white people go to tanning salons?"

"Cause they want to look like black people."

"If they want to look like us, then why do you say never trust whitey?"

"Cause white people want to look like black folk; they just don't want to be us."

"Why don't they want to be like us?"

"Because they don't want where we came from—from our heritage."

"Hmmm. What is our heritage?"

"They don't want to come from nuthin.'"

"Did our family come from nuthin'?"

"Everyday child. Everyday."

Addiction

The doctor said she had cancer of the lung. She bowed her head in sullen grief. She had always vowed to quit smoking soon and turn over a brand-new leaf.

He said her chance were one in three. She thought of her little ones at home. She latched her coat, went down the hall. Took out her cellphone and made the call.

She got in her car, wiped her eyes. Fired up her cherry corvette. Before she fastened her seatbelt, *she lit up a fresh cigarette!*

The Dance

We dance with the Lord. Sometimes close and sometimes far off. He wants a close dance. He wants to frolic and hold us close, yet we push Him away with our wrongdoings, our foibles, and our little self-oriented ways. In fact, it is very easy to push Him out, and a lot of the time we do it without even thinking about it.

We have our idols. We preoccupy ourselves with material things, which quite frankly, is easy to do. It is easy to love our new **BMW**, or **Gucci** shoes, or maybe a **Coach** purse or howabout the newest iPhone?

We get distracted like in the **Book of Haggai** where we build our paneled homes and forget who gave us the means to acquire such structures. We remember not that these are gifts, blessings, and a token of God's unrestrained grace.

Love is truly a four-letter word, spelled T., I., M., E. We forget to make time for the Lord, as do many parents with their children; the same is true for us with our friends and acquaintances. All He truly wants is us.

When we sin with wrongdoing He forgives absolutely. But do we apologize? God is person or persons, that is, with feelings. When we stumble, we push Him, block Him, and compromise our relationship. At times like this we indeed dance far apart.

Sometimes when this happens, we lose our peace—the *peace that passeth all understanding*. We get caught up in the world. Stressed out and wrapped up in frivolous daily proclivities draw us away from our Maker who really wants "Marys" more than "Marthas," if you will.

When we adore Him and others, we dance closely. When we forgive and are patient we dance closely. When we take time for others and yes, even ourselves, we dance closely. But a lot of the time, we just plain don't.

Israel ended up dancing far apart for centuries, and so came the young baby child to remind us how badly He wants to dance closely.

Let not forget. Amen.

God's Wrath

The other day I made a mistake. Small sin it was, yet I stumbled. God forgave and I apologized. Yet during that hiccup my peace was gone. He was far from me. I felt His brief, stewing anger percolating as He briefly hid His face.

With repentance came fresh dew. Thankfully, love keeps not record of wrongs. Yet there are consequence for my blunders for which I have remorse. Yet, these regrets are only overshadowed by the thankfulness for the grace and mercy from the One and Only who rights the bicycle whenever off it I fall. Learning from my mistakes I become more like Him, and even draw closer.

And that is all that matters.

The Machine.

Three times a week for four hours I am hooked up to that blasted machine—a dialysis machine. It saves my life, but reminds me how fragile my existence is, and how truly my days are numbered. I watch my blood flow in and out of the tubes in my chest and wonder how long will I suck air and see another sunrise?

Yet, there is peace and joy in frailty. As I stare at the beeping and buzzing machine pumping the life in and out of me, I know that He has provided a way for me to continue. Yes, it is onerous, but I am thankful.

Each breath I take is a gift. And until the ultimate healing, I shudder much in awe of the way He provides and makes do in my weakness so I can continue to serve, *even as the fallen soldier I am.*

The Hound

We all know the hound. He has no master, and unleashed forays through the dark streets at night. He forages through our garbage and salvages what is edible to survive one more day. He has no warm bed in winter, nor ready water bowl on hot steamy, sultry, days. He cannot help it; he is mangy, dirty, and yes, maybe a bit smelly too.

We glance at the mutt and peer closely to see if there is a collar. If not, we call the puppy police to rid us of this bother—this undesirable nuisance.

Yet in each of us there is a hound—a fractious bundle of insecurities and ineptitudes that makes us hate the stray. For all of us are strays on the run—from our jobs, our family, and yes, even ourselves. We stay busy just to forget we are only two paychecks away from being on the street ourselves.

So we laugh at the stray, just as we avoid the homeless and the infirmed. In our inmost places, we quiver, knowing full well, that all of us someday are bound for the nursing home, with dry slobber running down our faces. Tis like Poe's **Masque of the Red death**, in whom our own fate is apparent, and which we all much face and cannot avoid.

So, run dog run—*as must we!*

For the Children

Trisha looked the Welfare Administrator in the eye and firmly said,

"I don't want to divorce my husband."

"Look, Mrs. Reynolds, your husband makes too much. Right now, you do not qualify for benefits."

"So you want me to leave my husband of fourteen years?"

"Well, think about it. If you leave him, you get food stamps, a medical card, discounted gas and electric, and a free cell phone."

"But I love my husband."

"He can still live in the same house"

"But I made a sacred vow before God."

"Hun. Think of the children. You gotta put food on the table."

Trisha hung her head. Her eyes became moist.

"Don't you see Hun—the government is giving you a freebee. You're a fool not to take it."

Two days later she went to the County Courthouse and filed for divorce.

--so much for love, marriage, and balancing the Federal Budget

Running Sore

Loneliness is like a running sore. It smarts rightly, and drains woe for seemingly forever. Unless tended to, it never heals. Usually the wound is from solitude, but one can feel lonely, even if not alone. Lack of companionship is the enemy, but also loneliness strikes when one is not understood, minimized, or ignored—even in a crowd of people. Lack of affirmation is as deadly at times as isolation.

These last three years—10 surgeries and the amputation of the leg have left me homebound, isolated, away from work and far from my students, family, or friends. I have starved for contact with others and have learned the spanking hard truth about facing myself with a microscope—and not always liking what I see.

But lamentation doth end where the spirit still rejoices when one can still come hither to the Lord in times of abyss of alone time. Quiet moments stir the still sweet voice of the Lord, and the joy of an occasional bump or a word of knowledge. And, once in a while there is satisfaction from that tiny tap on the shoulder directing me to a cogent scripture verse or an important image brought to mind.

In the Old Testament, Joseph spent thirteen years in prison so my three must be Childs play. I hold fast knowing my Redeemer lives, and the simple truth that He indeed will bring this vacant, empty existence to pass, be it through others or my own reconciliation of a continued life of solitude meant to be.

All of us, who at times experience these extended periods of quietude, can reflect upon John Milton, who in anguish and repine beautifully penned, **"They also serve who stand and wait."**
Amen.

Hating God

It would be easy to hate God. I was a college professor who loved teaching. Daily striding into the classroom and opening minds with joy and mirth. Now, I am butchered. I have lost my leg, and my kidneys have failed. I can no longer practice the avocation I love.

Yet, I am blessed beyond all measure. I have a comfortable home, a warm cozy bed. I have a wonderful, caring, committed wife. I have stuff. Cars, computers, guitars, and of course—my doggies. I have a family, church, and friends. I have dialysis which keep my heart pumping which allows me to keep writing. Most of all, I have my Lord, who gives me the *peace that passeth all understanding*

It's not Pollyanna. It's recognizing that in God's tragedy is His mercy. He has placed me where He wants me to be—writing and worshiping Him in solitude. *I must be thankful.*

There is a book called ***A Severe Mercy*** where a man loses his wife but in doing so finds God and finds himself richly blessed; * this I understand and in my own circumstance celebrate what *Yahweh* has done to me. Job was blessed in spite of *"[A]ll the calamity the Lord brought upon him;"* his double recompense was wealth and being made whole. My wealth is in my knowledge of the Most High, and the coziness with Him never before experienced.

I cannot walk, work, or practice many things I love, but my spirit daily frolics with the One and Only as I will do for all eternity with peace and joy. I say, "Thank you Lord, for this relational tasty sneak peek, *and for giving me You, which is the sweetest thing of all."*

*Sheldon Vanauken, *A Severe Mercy* (1976)

Young Love

It was a clear summer evening on a clean swept porch. An eager, nervous young man bent to one knee. She clasped her hands upon her fresh, nubile face, shook her head, and said, "*No.*" It was snowy Christmas Eve, and another bent to his knee in front of this slim, fetching, high cheek-bone woman. She pulled her flaxen hair back, shook her head, and murmured, "*No.*"

One day, having just exited the **Piggly-Wiggly**, an enticing handsome man stopped her by her shopping cart. He asked her to the Saturday night movie. She stiffly buttoned her turncoat, and said, "*No.*"

Now in his fifties, Clarence, a distinguished divorcee, deftly popped the cork of **Tott's** champagne in his jet-black stretch limo. He looked to her, and smoothly popped the question. She calmly straightened her shawl, and politely replied, "*No.*" He pulled his thinning silver hair back, lit a Cuban, and asked, "Why?" "Remember Tommy Jamison?" She softly asked. He replied, "Yeah—wasn't he the guy from the gas station that left for South America to find fame and fortune? He used to work on my car."

" Well, he is coming back." "How do you know?"

"Because he promised." Clarence shook his head in disbelief and laughed raucously.

Now in her seventies she slowly trudged home. It was biting cold and raining. As she passed by the local Apothecary, a silver-gray **Rolls-Royce** pulled up beside her. The door opened slowly. A bent old frosty white-haired man got out and bent to one knee. She smiled, rearranged her gray hair, and with moist eyes nodded and said, *"Yes."*

It's true: grease monkeys always get the best girls

Sugar Daddy

"Damn it's cold outside!"

"Come on engine! Warm up!"

"Why is there so much frickin' traffic in the morning?"

"God knows I hate these red lights."

"It's raining. Crap! Where is my blasted umbrella?"

"That stinkin' restaurant be better open."

"Missy, my coffee is cold! "God I hate these slow, fat waitresses."

"Man, I don't want to work today in my crappy job. Maybe I will quit anyway."

'Mmmm. This orange juice is good! May I have another?"

"Nice hot grits. " Good grape jelly."

"Eggs are cold, and the toast is too dark, but that is okay—nobody is perfect."

"You know, come to think of it—the server is kind of cute."

"Huh. The rain has stopped. Looks like the sun is out."

"Man--that was a good breakfast. I gotta tell the manager!"

"Wow. I am late for work. I gotta get going—there are a million things I want to get done today."

"Yes—I know it's a big tip—keep the change, Sweetie." "Thanks for the lumber! (toothpick)."

With a smile, this **Metformin** man walked briskly out the café door.

Eye of the Needle

I watch the millionaires play hoops on T.V., and I wonder why college football coaches make twenty times more than our President—I see all this, and I smile. For me, I monthly deposit my small disability check. I think of many things I want and cannot have. Yet, as Sheryl Crowe croons, *"It's not having what you want—it's wanting what you got."*

"Better to be content with a little, than unhappy with a lot" the **Proverb** reads. Yet, it seems unfair. Why do some flourish while many suffer want and need? It's easy to envy with hungry covetous eye.

But manifest opulence can be dangerous. Having more physical things bring contentment, not peace, as well as masking spiritual growth and understanding. When we are right smug comfortable, we stop reaching for the unseen. Without the true blessing of the relationship with the One who made us, we are left easily wanting.

Lack brings need. Need brings want. Want asks for help. Eternal help can be provided. Perfect peace can be realized and garnered. Without need is the danger—the danger of never knowing or asking for help from Above and settling for stuff over spirit.

We die with toys, not the ticket never coming to understanding of the beauty and truth of the metaphysical joys provided in Him and His rich provision. Shiny cars do not preclude having Providence, but they may keep us from seeing the beauty and truth of the Maker. Sometimes having what we want keeps you from having what we should, and in that there may be very very long-term consequences. Thankfully, we have a merciful God who knows us, and understands us. But we should take heed, for as they say, *"Not to decide, is to decide."* (Think about it).

The Girl Next Door

We used to play in the sandbox. Monica had bright blue eyes and trim flaxen hair. Her brimming smiles were as wide as the Atlantic Ocean, and she flashed it 24-7. She grew up tall and strong. Smart, yet athletic. Dated the captain of the football team, to my chagrin. Once she was in college, she never really spoke to me again.

She married a soldier who went to Iraq who got blown up and developed P.T.S.D. He came home in pieces, somewhat patched together, but heard he was never right again. Monica, God bless her, stood by him, and nursed him back to full physical health.

Heard he'd get angry and liked to drink. Pummeled her one night unrecognizable. Cops came but was too late. They still lived next door when it happened, and I saw them take her out on a stretcher, bloody sheet and all. I heard it was a big funeral, but I couldn't face going myself.

I wept for months. She wasn't my girl, but I had badly wanted it to be so. On long, rainy nights or cool frosty morns when thinking too much, my minds turns to Monica—yeah, Monica and those days in the sandbox, and my sad eyes get moist every time.

Fear

Essentially the basis of all fear is the alarm or trepidation that occurs out of a concern or threat of losing something. We fear losing a loved one, or more recently, we might quake at the thought of losing our iPhone. In the scriptures the opposite of fear is love, for it says *perfect love drives out fear.* This is why to young lovers have no fear when, totally infatuated, they make promises they could never possible keep.

The *"rich young man"* in the Bible was asked to give up all his possessions in order to have *"treasure in heaven."* He chose not to do so, keeping his earthly goods over having a certain spiritual attainment. I think we all fear this to some extent. I ask myself, "By putting God first will I have to give up the house and two cars I personally possess?" The short answer is "no." Money is not the root of all evil, but rather the *love* of money is the detriment. Rich men do pass through the *"eye of the needle"* because the scriptures read *"[W]ith God all things are possible."*

This is not to say that an abundance of possessions or "stuff" doesn't distract or become an idolatry of sorts. We all know the guy who has four houses and ten cars and still it not satisfied; his insatiable hunger for earthly articles my blind or preclude him from ever being truly spiritually sated.

Yet I know people who fear developing faith in the fear they may have to give up their "stuff." Or they simply are not comfortable with the idea of something bigger than them, the upshot being one has to abide by someone else's rules. Much of this thinking resides in human pride and a desire for control.

Truth be known, you can have all the possessions one wants as long as it is kept in perspective. When you call Him Lord, you mean He is top dog, numero Uno. It is important to realize that what He says about what one can or cannot do or have is between Him and the individual. True the Bible is clearly normative, with explicit rights and wrongs—but God always take us where we are, and intimately works with us on *His timetable*. I smoked cigarettes as a Christian for over a decade before I felt that strong tap on the shoulder to quit, which I did.

Instead of being afraid of what one has to give up to come into relationship with the Maker, one might ponder what one gains. One acquires a relationship giving peace and life into perpetuity. Sounds like pretty good "stuff" to me, and far as giving up the **Lexus**? Let's just say I have never heard of my Lord letting a set of car keys stand in the way of any person's salvation. *Alleluia!*

Cattitude

Cats are smart. Cats are sneaky. Cats are independent. They are warm, fuzzy, and pliably lazy. They don't come when they are called, and they only visit you on their terms. Overall, they are mostly disloyal, and horribly secure in their own smarmy, immodest proclivities.

Cats have attitude—*Cattitude.* They sometimes fool us, coming up and rubbing themselves against our ankles and seeming to want attention. But truly they only are seeking joy and emotional satisfaction on *their* terms.

Picky finicky eaters; they make us spend a month's wages on different repasts to find just the one he or she might perhaps like to consume. After a meal they lick themselves like Sheba on a fluffy pillow 'til bath time is over—at best, only giving us sidewise scowl or an unsatisfying furtive glance.

You pick up a soft kitten and it squirms. It may allow a snuggle, 'cause it ain't a cat yet. It doesn't yet the feline truth, namely that cats choose affection on their specifications only. Cat's leave us always wanting for more. And that is their secret. They hook us with just enough attention to keep them around, but not enough to sate our emotional needs and wants.

So we bow down to the resolutely fulsome cat, and accept them on their terms. After a few strokes, they saunter away for their precious naps. If we wake them unexpectedly, they give an unabashed sultry look of disgust and disapproval. When this happens we apologize, and throw treats at them only to discover they aren't interested in them, or maybe they save them for a better time of their choosing.

In some ways, we are like cats. We want things our way—on our terms. And when we don't get what we want—a job, a raise, a friendship, we turn and walk away. Idle in feelings, we balk at commitment, and perhaps instead choose blasé infatuation instead of love.

Yeah, there is Cattitude in all of us. We were wired this way. Unfortunate. There is more to life than Skippy hodgepodge affections on the fly. But like the cat, we never stick around long enough to understand the truth—namely, that love comes from loyal, requited, reciprocal remonstrations of kept promises. Not just the fleeting hasty tasty rub.

Cat's teach us how not to be. Yet, we too often fall into the kitty truth and only look out for number one. And like cats, we may sit pretty all the lengths of our days, and die very very alone and lonesome. Unlike us, cats don't have regrets.

(That only we could be so fortunate).

In the Beginning

There seem to be three competing views as to how earth, man, and the Universe came to be. Creationism, as set out in the scriptures of the Bible holds an overall Deity responsible for all things. Intelligent Design argues *"Irreducible Complexity,"* namely, that our functioning systems could not have developed without any one or a number of requisite parts existing in the first place. Therefore, there must be some epistemological rationality to the Universe, although not necessarily God. The third type is Natural Selection, which argues that variations in genome or genetic mutation provides varying varieties of species that over time better adapt to a changing earth environment. Even with these gross oversimplifications here, it seems clear that each view precludes one another.

Yet, I would argue these views may not be a far apart as one seems. The non-theistic view says the earth could not be created in six days, but that assumes it is a person's day of twenty-four hours. What is a day for God when in the **Psalms** it iterates that day for the Lord is thousands of years? Arguments against Intelligent Design argue that biological complexity can exist and develop without a rational process, yet, this does not disprove but rather merely questions the theory's foundation. Some say Natural Selection may indicate a randomness in the species, and in species development, but that in itself is not proof of how the earth actually came to be in the first place, nor does it explain multitudes of species that seem to have not changed over time.

I believe the Bible to be true, yet not all truth is in the Bible. We can exegesis all truth out of the Bible by application, namely we can apply scriptural truths to any situation on earth and sky, but there isn't any mention in the Word of marshmallows, snowmobiles, or iPhone anywhere. My view is that you cannot fit all of God into a single book. The Bible is an ""owner's manual" of sorts in that all it contains is true.

Yet like with an owner's manual to fix many problems in a car, you may need to look outside its contents, say using diagnostics or a certified repairman. To reiterate the analogy, the owner's manual is all true, but not all truth about motorcars in the manual.

Likely I am wrong, but I am convinced that these three views are not completely mutually exclusive or incompatible. I start with God creating yet granting His creatures the ability to adapt to a changing environment for the sake of survival, just as we now today eat blueberries to avoid free radicals in order to combat the development of cancer cells. This is not incompatible with Intelligent Design, nor some of the tenets of Natural Selection.

When a baby horse is born, you don't immediately put a saddle on the foal and ride. You wait for it to mature and develop long before being rode and directed by its master. God spoke to Abraham at the appointed time and he heard and obeyed His voice and it was reckoned to him as righteousness. Timing is everything; one does not explain metaphysics to a four-month-old child. There is an intelligence to God giving His creatures the ability to learn, grow, think, and change over time. Far be it me to limit what He can do or try to understand all He can do.

True, these are onerous oversimplifications of these theories, yet who is to say God didn't plant in us all these seemingly conflicting ideas in the first place? Our inability to make such ideas compatible may have just been His plan from the beginning. *Don't forget about Babel.*

Small piece of Heaven

Late night. As thunder shudders, crickets ease their humming. Dog is in and doors locked. House as dark as molasses and quiet as a sepulcher. Just me. Wife is in Tuscan. I am lying on the couch next to my patio window—the kind with the sliding door. Feel the heavy air so thick I could swallow it. Light tap on the mobile home roof. More taps into a light staccato. It's raining. Warm inside; humid. *Real close.* I sit up and grope for my ice-cold soda on the coffee table. I slowly nurse the bevy letting the cool ice floating at the top tickle my nostrils.

I can see the green illumination of the clock radio across the room on the kitchen counter: **2:30 a.m.** I entertain a deep yawn, and relaxed, fall back onto the sofa like a sack of potatoes dropped onto the back of an old pickup truck. Gonna sleep in, so I turn off my cell phone; it's Friday night—mea culpa, Saturday morn.

I hear a car pull in next door and then, inebriated shouts to get indoors fast. I flash a cozy smile in dark. A soft summer rain, lightly pinging on the roof like plucked violins stings sooths my tired, worn out brow. I sigh for a moment thinking about the day at the mill—got no worries now. It's the weekend. Think I get my new rod and go to reservoir tomorrow and get me a mess of tasty pan fish. Bring 'em home and cook 'em up with lots of salt and thick butter. Mmmm. Maybe down a couple of cold ones too.

Eyes needing toothpicks, so I close 'em and drift off as the rain intensifies into a high lonesome wail. Before I slip off, I think of my old lady; I miss her, but kinda like having the whole place to myself. I smile and fall into a gentle dream world as soothing as one chewing on warm marshmallows.

I drift off, and dream pleasantries. The rain, now a deluge, pounds the roof like a passing freight train, yet no sound rouses me from the thick, deep slumber. Thankfully I oversleep, keeping the world out forevermore.

--a working man's small piece of heaven.

Shame

We all do things wrong, and at times, reprehensible. They say guilt is how you feel about what you did. Shame is how you feel about yourself afterward. Both are difficult, but the latter can last much longer even after repentance.

Deep shame makes us feel unworthy, unlovable, and at times, unforgivable. In fact, we may have asked for absolution, but to no avail. Our tail down, we still feel like that "*bad dog*," whimpering, with ears back, running to slide under the sofa. Nothing can mollify the deep wretched pain of regret pulsing in every cell of our beings.

Shame is not ephemeral, nor easily ameliorated, even after being forgiven. Like a bad penny, it keeps turning up, no matter what we do, deeply cutting the heart, mind, and soul like a jagged knife across our body, leaving an omnipresent scar of constant reminder at every turn. People who love us try to placate, assuage, or ease our pain—a kind word or a sloppy hug, yet perhaps to no avail.

Only by accepting ourselves as the imperfect, the human, and seeing that genuine regret means a piece of us is truly good or smacking of real virtuosity. Sincere remorse is the cue, the sign of a morsel of true righteousness. *Without goodness, one cannot feel bad.*

So, we scrape the warts off the dead skin of regret by understanding that we all fall and make mistakes—knowing that the only one to not ever misstep was a we guy nailed to a tree. We all muck up at times, even badly, or even at times, dreadfully.

We can try to make up for our errors—do some goodness to atone for our doddery. Yet, only in recognizing the eternal love given by pure grace from Above can we show mercy toward ourselves, and then perhaps, others.

Swallowing His charity, we drink in a deep sense of tasty relief and a sense of thankfulness for the pardon, which we all do have for the asking. Shame can be a monster—hard to put away. We tend to but tuck it in deep and sadly ruminate on it forever. Or we can deeply ingest the truth, namely, that only by forgiving ourselves can we free ourselves of the dread and regret that causes us rue. And as we excuse ourselves, the cool honeydew vine water of relief soothes our mind and soul and leaves us grateful just at the thought for a second chance—a "do over."

So gratefully, we finally move on, knowing how now to show mercy toward others, as we honestly understand our little spot in the simple place called humanity, where even a "*Charlie Brown tree*" can be made beautiful.

Selah

They Choose Us

Animals know us. They read our hearts. They scurry to us, with yelp or bark. They come close to those they trust. Caring folk are worth the fuss.

It isn't training or an advanced degree how animals discern one's pedigree. Generosity can't buy love or trust. Many treats bring incipient pleasure, but can't buy love, by any measure.

It is simply between a giver and a taker. A genuine hug, or a scanty rub behind the ears from a pet loving faker.

But in the end, we don't choose our pets. They choose us or send regrets. Animals, like children, don't want shallow time like old bones on a shelf. They simply want us to give of ourselves.

Best Soldiers

They say happiness comes from the world, peace from the spirit, and joy from the soul. But when things go south, it is easy to feel stressed, rankled, or distraught. When tragedy strikes our core is shaken or even obliterated. We claw for balance, emotionally tottering when we get the phone call from the State Highway Patrol about the accident, or the word from a doctor about our child with Big C.

As we reel and flounder, we must recalibrate. We scan the scriptures for a verse—something to make us feel better. But the Holy words cannot take the place of simply trusting in Him. He is there, not necessarily to make the situation go away, but to see us through it—be it with a better outcome or not.

"The scriptures say, *"He will not test us more than we can bear,"* yet, we have our moments of sheer excruciating, deleterious, noxious, agonizing emotional wreckage. At times like this we grope for resolution, consolation, and succor, hoping against hope for a solution in a sometimes-no-win situation we cannot sometimes control.

But only by giving up control can we gain control. When we give it to Him, we maintain our peace, our *Shalom,* our tranquility. Armed with this wholeness coming from His strength we hang on, and with His grit we get through and make it to shore, with or without the lifeboat. For He is our life preserver even when life squeezes our innards thin.

Truth be known, even hanging on Him we may not get the outcome, the resolution we want, but we get the result He wants; for even in abject tragedy there can be blessing—there may be a Divine sanction we at this time cannot or will not understand or comprehend.

So, we simply hold on based on this knowledge—an understanding that we don't deal the cards; we just play out our hand as best we can, and cope even when things get really crazy or untenable. As we recognize this, we keep our peace even when the crap comes down seemingly unfairly. Holding it together in the storm, we can more than tread water—*we can overcome regardless of outcome.* In doing so, we become survivors, and for that we are thankful. And with gratitude we gain new strength, and boldly trod on.

Tough times and obstacles *"suck,"* but they make us stronger. And like worn leather, the more berated we become, and as we suffer, the softer we can become, and more useful to the Maker. As C.S. Lewis once remarked, '*Wounded Christians make for God's best soldiers.*'

Conditional Love

We all know that God gives agape, or unconditional love. But what is hard to see, or even comprehend, is that He doesn't give unconditional favor. Love is based on true commitment. It does not change. However, favor, or preferential treatment is different.

It is easy to say that God doesn't show preferential treatment. Well, look at life: some people are rich; some are poor. There are those with disease or injury. Some get healed. Some do not. Some are famous and have it on the easy street. Others fight their whole lives struggling paycheck to paycheck. Some go to Vegas and make it big; others go broke and wonder why.

It says in the scriptures that the Angels and Heavenly Hosts sang, *"Glory to God in the Highest. Glory to God in the Highest. And peace to all those with whom He is pleased. Glory to God in the Highest."* Peace to all those with whom He is pleased? Hmmm. It seems a bit unfair indeed.

In fact, it seems really unfair—until we realize that God is a person, or persons, and He can and do what He pleases. I mean, isn't that true with us? We choose to please ourselves. Besides, God *is* God. Who are we to argue? Okay. So how do we get God's favor? Truth is—we can't. It has to come from Him. Well, can we do all the right things? Ya know, try and butter Him up? Ya know, like try and be good all the time? Truth be known, we can do things to please Him, namely by giving Him worship and reasonable obedience, yet, these things should be an end in itself—not a ploy to get our way, if you will.

In the end it is all His grace, or unmerited favor; this is something we cannot earn or make Him do. If He is to give us "merited favor," (If such even exists), that is His call only, and that truly boils down to His mercy. God is good—we know that. But life can be so hard and bad at times.

Unfortunately—or fortunately, depending on how we look at it—He gives us free will. We need to give Him that also. Full stop.

Just as we love our parents, we know that their blessings to us need to come from them on their terms. Sure, we may try to please them at times to get things we want, but trying that too much, too hard, or too often tends to do us little good, or maybe even backfires.

Trying to get in good with the Maker is never a mistake. But insipid duplicity to get what we want probably won't get us very far. He tends to have a good idea of what we are really thinking. It is hard to pull a fast one on The Almighty.

So, forget about buttering up The Big Guy. Just hit your knees and thank Him come what may. Let Him do the blessing. Hate to say it, but it is the only way. Otherwise, we end up trying to earn "*brownie points*" instead of having the simple joy of love and heartfelt service. And think about it—would we really want it any other way? Doubtful.

So, ask, pray, and serve. And most of all, be thankful. *We do have an eternal place in the sky*

Public Bath

The room and walls wholly lacquered. The kids in bed, truly knackered. We spread the blankie, old and tattered. Decided the meal, not worth mattered. Candlelight, tele, and the drum of rain, made us more smitten, so unashamed. We unfrocked slowly, sly smiles inane, ran to loo, and plugged the drain.

Tub soon brimmed, so we stepped in. Bath, bubbles on all sides hemmed us in. We slowly soaked in a week worth of sweat, with lugubrious moisture, warm and wet. From tub to sheets, we nibbled eats, Took to the dressing like a Sunday school lesson. In the bedroom, where we discovered—twenty years married, yet still lovers.

In the midst of passionate throes, we soon forgot our working-class woes. Yet at the climax of the rub, we 'membered our checkbook left at the pub. So we split for a few, oh God what a pain. She munched on roast as I left in the rain. When I returned the food was gone, but with randy smile we resumed the fun.

We kissed and played 'til dawn did break. Poor we were, but frolic did make. Promises made and promises kept. Penthouse not, but not one regret.

No Panic in Heaven

Life is tough, with many woes, regardless how much our storehouse flows. Many bucks don't ease the pain, when tragic blows come with disdain. We kid ourselves with senseless chatter. Never grasping what really matters. When crap comes down and hurts the fam—perhaps child in danger, our emotions slammed.

No way to measure the worry or blame, what's done is done, we fret insane. We shake our fist, with anger true, not knowing what to do. To lose a love is travesty, but in the end we come to see. Through it all, when woes doth leaven, we hold fast—*no panic in heaven.*

As the chips fall badly, we may grieve sadly, but in the end, we come to see, *His will be done, come eternity.*

Unwanted Return

Cold clammy limbs with rigor coming in. Body in a heap by the side of the drenched thoroughfare. Eyes barely fluttering. Reaching out with last gasp for passing headlights. Car stops with engine running. Door swings open. Quick footsteps and loud exclamation, "Jesus God!"

Sirens above the accident. Blue blackness. At first cold—very cold. Bright lights in face. Pumping chest. Masked folk jabber frantic. All becomes dark.

Drift she does above the scene. A peaceful feeling so serene. Without warning she is sucked back into her body. "Nooooo!" She blurts, "It's warm up here!"

*Heart monitor picks up. Now back in her cold, frigid body. She would not forgive God. Not for what happened, but for sending her back. As she slipped back into unconsciousness, she heard a still, small voice utter, "**Now you will live for my purposes.**"*

With eyes now closed, she fell fast asleep knowing full well the meaning of His will be done at any cost.

Mon Amie—a Tribute

My wife Janie is my best friend; my truest friend and confidante. After the first ankle surgery I slipped into a coma for four weeks. Endless nights she spent in her van in the hospital parking lot, so she could be near me 24-7.

She has taken me everywhere for the past three years as I have been unable to drive. Over seventy trips to Columbus to see doctors or the hospital—a trip of which is an hour away. All my decisions ran through her, and she supported me all the way—even losing my leg. Never letting me go to a nursing home following my surgeries, she took me and home and always took care of me.

Even though we have been through so much, she can still make me laugh. Just a sly look or a throw away one liner. She gets on me when I get down at times, reminding me how blessed I truly am. Not always needing to speak, she talks with her eyes, and usually has the last word.

The say angels have wings. My angel has rings, and they are mine and they are on her fingers.

Amen.

Pain

The last three years have been difficult. Ten surgeries and pain out the ying-yang—especially after the amputation. Yet pain can be good. It reminds us how fragile we are, and that in the final analysis we are nothing more than a random mass of protoplasm.

Pain can take many forms. Physical pain is more easily understood, and perhaps the most common. Yet, pain can also be from the mental, to the emotional, and even the spiritual. We all know what it is like to be on one's last nerve or simply to be at a loose end. Then there is the pain or hurt when one is wronged, or worse, when we lose a loved one. For whatever reason, sometimes our spirits are grieved mightily, be it through loss or other tribulation.

The best part of pain is when it abates or goes away. Not just by pill or drip, like after surgery, but in forgiveness, empathy, understanding, and compassion. Emotional burdens resolved lift the spirit, and turn rain clouds into calm, cool, crisp morning sunrises. And as pain recedes, there is thankfulness, relief, and even at times, joy, as well as peace with emotional healing. In times like this we rejoice.

For some situations, there may not be a cure. Pain may drag on, ruthlessly. Or we have a twitch in our giddy-up that just won't go away. Regardless, pain reminds us more than anything else our humanity. The time clock is always ticking, and pain can be a horrible harbinger—a reminder of our limited time walking on planet earth.

I am older now. With my infirmities pain for me is a way of life. Yet I am still grateful. I remember how I used to run and jump in my youth. The golf and tennis games. The hiking and fishing trips. I can look back and be thankful. For now, as barely ambulatory, I see my life as having been full and fruitful. When alone, especially at night, I dream of earlier, healthier days, and with eyes moist—I remember.

Holidays

Holidays are funny—not funny "ha ha," but funny strange. We love the food at Thanksgiving, and gifts at Christmas. The Easter Bunny brings chocolate eggs in the springtime, and everyone loves Trick-or-Treat come October.

But then there is seeing family. We love to see our kinfolks, b*ut do we really like it?* Regardless of how we get along at the surface, there are always those little undercurrents. Why does my father have to have that smelly after dinner cigar, or why does my sister always pick on the food on the table before it is served? Why don't we ever speak of Grandma, just because we have left her alone in a nursing facility while we are at home having a family feast?

Then there are those emotional scars that never seem to heal that no one talks about, be it divorces, parental neglect, or the simple negative ruminations of being the middle child. Some children never feel good enough, and parents never feel understood or even respected. Grandparents are to be put up with and babies always having to be put down at the least possible opportune time.

Yepper, holidays are never easy, and frankly, almost a relief when over. The worst part being when once back home, we have to go back to work as tired as we were when we had our first day off. But we carry on with good cheer. For regardless of whether we enjoy or loath our family get-togethers, our holidays mark or chronicle certain times in our lives we cannot ignore. We put up with Grampa, and even poke fun at him behind his back, but when he is gone forever, there is a gaping hole in our heart. Holidays will never be the same without him.

So, cherish your holidays. We never know when they will be our last. And who will be missing at the next?

The Myth

Some say monogamy is a myth. Yet even in the animal world there are species of males and females completely loyal and make each their only. Some of those in this classification are swans, wolves, and coyotes, and even certain fishes. Scripture is chock full of references to the need for the marriage bed to important, sacred, holy and to be *"undefiled."* We live in an age where it seems we switch out our partners as oft as one would change pitches in a baseball game. I too, am guilty as charged, for I am divorced and remarried.

In the Bible Moses granted divorce under duress. For us, however, separation of man and wife is almost as easy as ordering a value meal at McDonalds. Marriage vows seem more like suggestions, rather than sacred promises.

It's funny. People ask me how long I've been married, and I respond, "Fourteen years." They reply, *"Congratulations!"* as if somehow that length of a continual nuptial is some sort of miracle. Truly this is a sad commentary when marriage is an institution that is simply an anachronism—something horribly out of date.

True love, I do believe exists, but it is about commitment and not idle infatuation or just based on salary or comeliness. Love is a daily decision more about who washes the dishes or takes out the rubbish. It's funny. My wife married a college professor. She ended up sticking with an amputee on dialysis three days a week. Yet, she has stood by me through the whole rotten nine yards. I think it doth not possible I could have been more fortunate.

They say love is a not a thing, but a verb. And the little daily doing is everything—that and that little promise that says, *"for better or worse."*

Life Preserver

*I was big. I was huge, tanking in at five hundred and fifteen pounds. Smoking two packs a day. I was heart attack waiting to happen. I tried quitting with the patch and with **Chantix**, but to no avail. One day deep in prayer I heard the voice of the Lord clearly say, "**Jack, you got to quit smoking.**" I stupidly asked "Why?" He calmly replied, "**Because it will affect the way your life will play out.** That day I put the cigarettes away forever. I have not had a cigarette now in over ten years.*

*I had tried to lose weight—at least I thought I had. I was furious at God because I felt He wasn't helping me enough to dock the pounds. One day I groused nastily toward the Lord, "Why can't You help me lose weight?" The Lord replied, "**Why should I do for you what you can do for yourself?**" Humbled and with new illumination, I embarked with new vigor, and I lost nearly two hundred pounds over a three-year period. Having done so, I feel much better despite my recent maladies.*

*I have no idea why the Lord spoke to me so clearly. I just know how badly I needed to change my lifestyle and eating habits. In hindsight, I was a fool the way I treated my body. In scriptures it says that "**The body is the temple of the Holy Spirit**," and thus holy. In that sense, I transgressed markedly.*

*Looking back, the Lord was my life preserver. There must have been something He wanted me to do for Him—to accomplish. I am still figuring out what that actually might be. I think that is true for all of us. We all have a special purpose on earth that no one else can do. For me, now as my health has indeed declined, He has put me in a position where I can only do one thing: write. So I do so in the hopes that when I pass I hear those words, "**Well done good and faithful servant.**" This I seek, and in doing so, I obtain His* *peace and joy. Eternity comes at a price, for which He paid and for which I inherited simply by the asking.*

In some ways the Lord's intervention was a test of obedience; one that I am still learning. I just know that when Lord speaks, I had better heed.

And so, I live and as directed, I write

The Rattler

Rattle snakes are grossly misunderstood. True, they are dangerous to us humans, but at least they warn us with a rattle. In actual life we rarely get a caveat or a warning for anything, be a mugger's .38 caliber or a startling letter out of the blue from the I.R.S. We cross our T's and dot our I's. We have our health insurance and maybe even an attorney on retainer, or at least a best friend of a friend who has passed the Bar. We may even have flood insurance in a non-flood zone or that silly extended warranty on our new television set.

Regardless, it always seems like something bites us in the derriere when we least expect it. It could be something pecuniary like a having to pay for a blown head gasket, or something more dear like when the medical test comes back positive (*as I have learned*).

So we go to plan B. Or plan C. The existentialist might claim it is all due to an individual's bad choices, but sometimes cause and effect isn't that clear. Nor is always a sure bet what is best to do come misfortune. Even if we consumeth a multitude of blueberries to stave off those free radicals, we still may end up on chemo. Even if jam down low sodium, low fat, and low cholesterol eats and we do beaucoup crunchers at the gym, we still might need bypass or a couple of stints. Yep, it as they say, "*It's always something.*" The problem is when it is us. *Probability doesn't matter much when we are the one.*

Yes, the rattlesnake has his rattle, and at least he gives us that warning. For this we should be thankful. He is thankful too, for in many cases, *his bite ends up his demise as well.*

The MRS

Economists called it the Marginal Rate of Substitution, or the less you have of something, the more you value it. This is true for life in general, for we always seem to want the things we cannot have. It may be material substantive things like that new iPhone, or elusive metaphysical things like love---regardless, we thirst plenty for which we much doth do not have.

And when we get things we want, we tend to then go for the upgrade, be it to a more idyllic person or to the newest late model **Porsche**—we always seem to want more. Never duly sated, we are like hamsters running on the circular treadmill of life. Sadly, almost only by exhaustion or limited budget do we settle in and make do with what we've got.

But there is a finer way. One of truth, contentment, and peace; we find this when we see things as gifts and privileges, not necessarily rights and entitlements. When we view our possessions as charity given or endowment rather than requirements, we can be thankful, and see that many times less is more.

The simple folk say, "Waste not—want not." Maybe they are not simple but wise, for in lacking they may see plenty, or perhaps just make the most of what they have. Like the **Proverb** reads, *"Better to be glad about little than unhappy with a lot."*

People like Trees

People are like Trees. Some are soft like white pine, whilst others are hard and tough as ironwood. But methinks it difficult to sometimes tell the difference. Some people like trees are soft or scruffy on the outside like birch. Other folk, like oak are tough all the way through. Many times, the grouchiest, meanest seeming people actually have the kindest hearts when we give them a chance. People are not born mean usually; they become mean for a reason. When we look past the bristle, we may see beauty. When we ignore the ill-mannered impertinence, we may see inner bloom or polish. Even Shelley's *Frankenstein* liked the delicate flower petals—should we not also see fragrance in people despite their multitude of foibles?

Let's not say odd but eccentric. Let's not say fat but of good appetite. Let's not say old but of good age. Let's not say ugly, but just perhaps aesthetically challenged. Let us not say slow of thought, but rather just methodical. It just takes time and effort to see the beauty on the inside. The sea urchin is a prickly, spiny, dangerous creature on the outside, but has become a sweet eating delicacy on the interior. We do choose to relish the inside sweet meat of the snail, calling it escargot, yet we forget to see how hard the outside shell of this gastropod is. Does anyone ever eat the outside of a simple banana?

Take heed: people are like trees. And like the beauteous palm that may bend and bow in melodious breezes—it has the roughest shoddiest bark of all. We would all be best served to give brash folk the benefit of the doubt, and look to heart, and perhaps spirit, for we each of us is special, unique. We may find that the deeper inside we look, the more we like. The more we like, the more we may love.

End note: Sometimes people are like wine that take time for succulence to be savored. The more secure we are, the more we can wait on the grape, if you will. In doing so, we all will be the richer, and there will less raison to whine…

Sullen Sunbeam

I have a cute, sleek jet-black little **Sunbeam** microwave oven. It is right smart on the outside, but it is sad, sullen on the inside. Even though aesthetically pleasing to the eye, it is only a 700-Watt unit—wimpy as microwaves go. *My Word!* It takes seven minutes to cook a **Lean Cuisine,** let alone nine minutes for **Banquet Hungry Man** meal. When it comes to defrosting nearly anything, it is just shy of pathetic. It is good with easy stuff like muffins or hamburger buns but can barely fight its way out of a boil-in-rice bag. To cook up a cup of hot water to a boil it takes an agonizing two minutes. Most embarrassing of all is the time it takes for a frozen **Stouffers Lasagna**—I mean we are talking twelve to fifteen minutes tops. Arrrrrgh!!

When I was a kid, we had some rich neighbors who had the real McCoy—an ***Amana Radarange***. This thing was huge and pulled so many amps it caused their kitchen lights to flicker when turned on. I mean it would destroy a hot dog in less than sixty seconds, and it made short work of any meat dish, from a steak to even a stout pork roast. It was a proud, boxy, and arrogant silver chromed microwave, bossy at heart and harboring few regrets for food it pulverized.

I never said anything to the ***Amana,*** but I saw it overcooking every meat dish. Yep, the food cooked from inside out leaving little but dry, dehydrated, bland, jerky-like viands. It would dry out any bun or make a biscuit as hard as a rock. It also had a highly irritating high-pitched whine like a one of those mini-vacuums that we use to sweep car interiors. And worst of all, if you covered a dish too snug, the oven would cause the contents to explode making a ubiquitous nasty mess.

Ya know, I know my little **Sunbeam** microwave oven is small, slow, and horribly insecure. But it is *special* in its own right—truly an overachiever for its size. True, the oven is a bit challenged, and probably will never headline **Consumer**

Reports, but I can be proud of it for giving a maximum effort every time. And to its credit, 'ol 'Beamer never overcooks any food. And best of all, this little microwave-that-could cost only sixty bucks. *Amen to that!*

You know, in the end microwaves are not that different from us humans. We come in all shapes, sizes, with different levels of power. But like these ovens, the best ones may be the meek humble ones that simply do what they are told, and not telling others what to do or where to go. True, the big, cranky, powerful ones are worth beaucoup bucks, and can make food go super nova, but can they heat up a cupcake without nuking the icing? Doubtful.

The scriptures say little about microwave ovens, but to hazard a guess, I think my little sullen **Sunbeam** might not too snazzy but might just be a shoo-in to slip through the appliance *eye of the needle. Hey little sullen **Sunbeam**—you go girl!*

Lonely Scarecrow

Goin' just up Rte. 36 past Centerburg village is a barren old cornfield blanketed in frozen field; it harbors a forlorn, sullen, lonely scarecrow. Clothing tattered and with emaciated arms and body, he is spilling straw and his faded black pantaloons shod no feet. His face is compromised with one button eye and broken twig for a nose. A painted on pedestrian frown is faded into a sidewise scowl as the years of dripping precipitation has won the war. A grungy spotty old gray chapeau completes the hen-pecked composite of a broken man currently out of a job.

Yet, the scarecrow's broad shoulders are square, and his elegant neck proud. Still sporting a crusty corncob pipe and a real, but faded pea-green **Johnny Walker** sport coat, he is stylin' in the snow.

The scarecrow's arms are outstretched like an illustrious, spirited preacher laying down the truth to a noisy gaggle of jet-black grackles. His wan, worthy head tilted off center splits the sky asunder, and the wicked wind ruffles his jacket making a light thwopping sound as my car drives by.

As I look back and see him fade slowly into the distance, I feel remorse for never having personally known this scarecrow in his prime. Yet, in the end, he has the upper hand, for unlike me, he is just seasonably unemployed; come spring he will be back in the action.

Wistfully, I benignly continue my lonely ride down the empty motorway into the evening dusk. I look back, and wave farewell to the lonely scarecrow now in the distance. But I grin knowing he probably is happier and personally more secure than I will ever be,

Why Weeping?

A learned person once asked me, "Why did Christ weep at Lazarus' tomb?" I responded because Lazarus was dead." He then pointed out how since Christ knows all things, and since He knows He will soon bring Lazarus back to life—why in the world would He be shedding tears? In fact, wouldn't He be rejoicing?

Duh! It hit me hard in the cognitive solar plexus. I realized this fellow's point. Jesus did weep at Lazarus' tomb not because Lazarus was dead, but because He felt the pain, sorrow, and loss that the other mourners at the tomb felt for their fallen friend and brother at the moment.

This is truly a seminal point, for it reminds us that even though God knows all things and all eventual outcomes, He still is in the ring with us—*He feels our pain and joy as we do.* This understanding reminds us that God is a person, or persons. He has his own set of feelings, and that He feels with us and for us.

So, as we walk in His will, we can take heart, for our Lord and Savior is the Living God. At our darkest hour He is there, which is a comforting and consoling thought. In time of rejoicing, no doubt He celebrates at well.

Truly, we are not alone.

Dry Season

When I was in my early teens my youngest sister was born. Some baby's cry a lot; this sister was no different. A number of times even as my sister grew older, when she would cry in the next room, my mother would not immediately go running pick her up or see what was wrong. When asked why she waited, my mother replied, "The child has to come to terms with situations herself—when I eventually come to her, she will learn to trust me in the absence. She will learn that I am there even when she cannot see me."

We all face dry seasons in our faith. It says in the scriptures at times God "*hides His face.*" Yet this is to our benefit. By protracted dry spells we learn two things. First, we need to stand on our own two feet and with faith proactively solve whatever issues face us. Two, we learn that God is there even when it feels like He is not there, and in doing so we learn to trust Him.

God doesn't want to jerk us around. No, He would rather teach us His ways, and guide into being able to do much for ourselves. Ironically, the more He teaches us, the less we may feel His presence in our daily lives because we will naturally act out in ways that is in His will. With no need to keep codling us, we may feel like we are in a dry season, but only because now He trusts us and knows we can make so many decisions for ourselves. As we mature in our faith, He still gives us bumps and little taps on the shoulders at times, but not perhaps as demonstratively as He does in our early Christian walk. Hence, at times we may feel a dry season, but many times it just means we are on the right course and He is trusting us. It is only when we may get off course He may more overtly intervene.

When making a dinner date with a good friend, all you have to say is when and where. Even if the event is two weeks away, if the friend is good enough, little more needs to be said; you know they will show up. --*it is the same with God.*

Propitiation

Propitiation—by definition *to cover*. Originally it meant the lid on the Ark of the Covenant. For us, it means the covering and wiping out all our wrongdoings. It is the basis of the "mercy seat" where our sweet Lord forgives and justifies us through faith. *By His stripes we are healed.*

We all make mistakes and blunders. When I have done so, I can only ask forgiveness, and say *"Thank you,"* for I know His sacrifice atones for my wrongdoings. For this I cannot fathom the depth of His love, nor understand the pain of his sacrifice.

On a different note, a lot of people have problems with this *God becoming man* thing, which is understandable. To me it is kind of simple. It isn't just His taking away of all our wrongs that amazes me, as it is the message of love provided by His coming in the first place. What scares me is His humility, dropping down from the heavens to become one of us, even just for short time. It was the only way to get our attention—to tell us face to face how much we are treasured from Above when the scriptures seemed to have run dry and prophet after prophet had been ignored.

It is easy to ignore Him. Life is busy and gets in the way, for as Wordsworth truly penned the" *[W]orld is too much with us."* And we too, like Him, get lost in the shuffle. It's almost funny—in actuality we learn how our rare quiet times are as much for us as they are for Him.

In the end it is just going to be and Him and us anyway, so what's the big whoop? Depends on how we look at it. Let's just say that time with Him may be well spent, for relationally, He for me is as much the trip as He is the destination.

They say heaven on earth isn't possible. I say heaven despite earth is possible, for those like me who are imperfect, yet forgiven

Asbestos Land

Bang-bang! Guns are everywhere. Folk shooting up schools, bars, nightclubs, and even churches and synagogues. Frustrated, angry, and hateful people expressing themselves with bullets instead of banners. Unspeakable horror as innocent lives are lost, and it seems little can be done to put these crimes to a halt. Evil seems to be winning.

Where is God in these tragedies? First, He is angry. Second, He is weeping. Third, we know these perpetrators if unconfessed end up in the land of asbestos. Yet, that is little consolation for those who are lost or have lost loved ones.

Too many dying and too little done. He is watching, weeping, and shaking His angry fist. Regardless, it is up to us to stop the madness. We must be aware of the reality of angry people with military-grade weapons. Show love when it hasn't been shown. Scriptures say to '*overcome evil with good.*' Hard to do when guns are as available as **Hershey** bars.

By identifying the distress in folk, we have a chance. It may be as simple as giving a pair of shoes or a hot meal. To "stand" in the evil day may be more of spreading God's love than arming more teachers in the classroom.

Having said this before, these tragedies are not God's purpose; but it is up to us to make them purposeful. It's not what happens, but how we respond to it. Where wrongdoing abounds—*grace abounds even more.* Let us fight fire with fire by spreading love, commitment, and understanding; it is the only way.

Embracing darkness in the little ways head-on may difficult and challenging, but not doing so may indeed be far worse.

Amen.

God's People

I once heard a preacher talk about when St. Paul of Tarsus was on the road to Damascus and was blinded by God who said, *"Saul, Saul, why thou persecuting Me?"* The upshot of the sermon was that God was saying that when Paul was killing multitudes of Christians, he was indeed really wounding God Himself.

The implication of this is far reaching, for it means when we hurt, malign, or belittle others, we are truly hurting God. This makes sense for each one of us is perfectly crafted by God down to the tiniest hairs on our heads. In our own way, each of us carries the face of God—just as our Lord said to the Pharisees regarding the face on the Roman coin, namely, *"Give to God which is God's, and give to Caesar what is Caesar's."*

These days there is a push to eliminate "bullying" for younger children. It seems to me we need to stop "bullying" people of all ages. Hurting or demeaning others obviously subverts the *Golden Rule,* but just as cogently, it demeans and harms us, the perpetrators. It comes back on us. As it says in **1John**: 3:15: *"Anyone who hates his brother is [at heart] a murderer and you know that no murderer has eternal life within him."*

On the flip side, any smallest gesture of kindness is to one's credit, and is good to the giver. As we know, *"As you give so shall you receive."* Even more so, greater tenderheartedness toward others is a thing of beauty. As Emily Dickenson wrote, *"If I can stop one heart from breaking, I shall not live in vain."*

Perhaps if we were kinder and gentler more Dickenson's would stay around

Backpack Blues

It has been said that when one carries unforgiveness (if that is a word) in their heart, it is like carrying a backpack loaded with large stones. It weighs the person down with anger, resentment, and regret. It can be deleterious when people hold grudges, even when they may have been hurt in a multitude of ways, be it physically, mentally, emotionally, spiritually, or sexually. One has a right to be angry when wronged. Anger is not the issue. It is what one does with one's anger that matters. The concern here is that when one does not forgive it holds one captive to a range of ill emotions that just are not healthy. Such folk are left to find other means to cope with their hurt or anger that may not be particularly helpful.

I suffered serious wrong in my younger days and I took it out on food, drink, and cigarettes. Yet, when I forgave the persons that wronged me, *I ended up the winner*. For each person I forgave, my backpack of hurt, resentment, and anger got that much lighter. When one forgives from the heart, it releases you, the victim, from being captive to all the emotional junk that goes with the wrong. Once you start the forgiving process, you eventually lose the backpack altogether and you find a new sense of freedom. By letting go of the resentment and hurt you make room for joy, and also a new-found sense of peace and tranquility. You exhale hate (and even self-hate) and breathe in more acceptance for the harmer and oneself.

Sometimes it is very very hard to forgive. This is especially true if the person who wronged you does not come forward to ask for forgiveness. But the trick is not basing the forgiveness on them asking for it. Sure, would be nice is all trespassers would say they are sorry, but that doesn't always happen. One almost needs to deal with the unrepentant others in a selfish way—to pardon them anyway to free oneself of the burden of the ill emotions of the wrong. Forget about them apologizing and be free. Move on. Don't let their wrong control you and make your life miserable. It is almost a form of self-healing, really.

The people that I suffered wrong were unrepentant, yet I forgave them. In doing so I was able to drop the overuse of food and drink. I became much physically healthier because I was happier on the inside. Eventually I put the cigarettes down as well, and that improved my health dramatically. With forgiveness I no longer needed the crutches that were really a form of bondage.

Finally, when one forgives from the heart, one almost ends up pitying the person of wrong. One can see their fragilities and realize they may be hurting too. Then compassion comes into play, and then in some ways, by doing so, we become completely healed from the original hurt.

God says to *pray for you enemies*. Part of that may be through forgiveness. In doing so, you, the forgiver ends up the winner. With resentment gone, joy and peace prevail.

So if you need to forgive others, what is stopping you? Be good to yourself. Be of good cheer. Backpacks are waiting to be lightened everyday

Photo Album

When one looks at a large photo album at times, he or she may see many different pictures of the same person. Some happy, sad, pensive, etc. Each photo is a snapshot of a person's disposition at a particular moment. And within each shot usually there is a context, be at home, on vacay, or really anywhere. The point is that the character of the person in the photo usually shines forth within the particular setting they are in as well as the circumstances surrounding them.

The same is true for God in the Bible. We see Him in a zillion different situations and see how He behaves. We see what He says and what He does. In doing so we can glean the character of the Lord. We understand some of His personality or personalities.

What we see in the scriptures is a God with a diverse range of feelings and moods. He can be a *"consuming fire,"* or like with Elijah after the earthquake, a God coming forth as a gentle breeze. Generally speaking, the scriptures say the Lord is kind, loving, and compassionate, slow to anger and quick to forgive. Over and over we see that He is *"with you always,"* yet in **Isaiah** as in other places in the Bible is says God at times *"hides His face."* He is kind and gentle in that *"a bent reed He will not break not a smolder wick He will no snuff out."* In **Matthew** it says *"His yoke is easy and His burden is light."* In **Hosea** God is ever so forgiving of Israel's abject waywardness or *"backsliding."* Yet, in **Hebrews** it says it is a *"dreadful thing to fall to the hands of the living God,"* with regard to unrepentant backsliding Messianic Jews. His anger is clear toward anyone who hurts children, for to such perpetrators He says *"it would be better off if they had never been born.* Yet, clear forgiveness and mercy is show in **John** where the Lord pardons the woman caught in the act of adultery. He says many times He is a *"jealous"* God and one to be "feared," yet at the same time He is the gentle, protective shepherd that we see in **Psalm 23**. He is a constant rescuer like in **Daniel,** and a redeemer as in **Job**. Yet He can punish as He did by taking David's first-born child when David *"went"* with Bathsheba and essentially killed her husband Uriah by putting him on the front lines in battle. He is also a deliverer, as it says in **Isaiah** where *"When you pass through the waters, I will be with you through the fire you will not be burned."* In this book He also shows His love and commitment for where He says in verse 4: *Because you are precious in My sight and honored, and because I love you, I will give men in return for you peoples in exchange for your lives."*

So like a photo album, the Bible shows the many faces and the character of the living God. Through these scriptures we can not only better believe in God—*we can know Him*. And it is clear He has feelings. Finally, through the Gospel it is clear He wants a relationship with us; *whether we take Him up on it or not is purely up to us.*

Alabaster Blanket

Sitting at my desk and above my green computer screen I look out my frosted kitchen window. It is winter in Ohio, and the usual gray wet days have been surprised by a heavy snow. The ground outside my house lays out like a serene virgin alabaster blanket, save for some heavy footprints by the base of my white trim garage. It is deathly silent. Even automobiles traversing the back alley just whoosh by with tires noiselessly pushing through the eight-inch snow. No birds—not even a lonesome snow dove to keep me company.

By contrast, the stark dark trees loom over my neighbor's green shuttered house reaching to the heavens—their branches little spindly fingers trying to clutch the gunmetal gloomy sky. Jagged icicles hang off the gutters and prickly point downward spiny like White Sea urchins hiding on the underside of a craggy coral reef. Peering farther out I see my neighbor's silver mid-size **Toyota** sitting in her drive with thick chunky ice encrusted up under front tire walls; the windshield is frosted with a translucent thick coating. Her headlights look almost sad, barely peeping out through accumulated snow over the front black trimmed bumper.

I stop looking out the window and take a long drink from my steamy mug of **Swiss Miss** hot chocolate that my wife just slid my way. I've got the smooth musical tones of classical 91.1 FM pumping softly through the room. My furry terrier-mix mutt is lying lights out silently at my feet. The whole kitchen still smells of fried bacon from the morning repast an hour ago. As I nurse my hot chocolate, I notice the little melting marshmallows are floating about in the drink like tiny ocean buoys in a dark ocean spume. The hot beverage lightly burns my taste buds, but still is worth savoring as it drains down my throat and gently warms my whole upright carriage.

I smile. It's a Level Two snow emergency today and no one is going anywhere; *to be honest, that is perfectly fine with me.*

Silly Lilly

Lilly Blankenship left her orphanage at the age of eighteen and got a job washing dishes at the local small-town diner. Tall, gangly, she walked with a slight limp form childhood polio. With a slight speech impediment, she was taciturn unless spoken to which was a rare occasion. Her coworkers poked fun at her for her secondhand clothes and plain homely appearance. Whilst others were munching together in the breakroom, Lilly ate her lunch alone in the dish room. They called her Silly Lilly because she never took breaks nor vacations. She carried a small **Gideon** Bible in her apron and could be caught reciting verses as she worked the dish tank. On Friday nights the diner would host the local city 4-H governing body for a sit-down dinner. All diner employees attended but Lilly was never invited. After the restaurant closed Lilly did the requisite janitorial work, cleaning and mopping the floors. They always left the dirty grill for her to scrub and the coolers to stock. She alone was responsible for sweeping and cleaning the restrooms. On weekends when the diner was resupplied, Lilly alone unloaded truck and put away all the new stock. She would then break down the cardboard and carry it out with the rest of the trash for the week. Day in and day out she worked her fingers to the bone.

Forty years later the town was still going strong as was the diner, although the restaurant had changed hands. About this time Lilly died alone in her sleep in a small ramshackle trailer at the far edge of town. Only the local preacher came to her funeral. However, the justice of the peace who was the executer of her will called the whole town together the night she died for an emergency meeting. The whole crowd packed into local high school gym. There was a buzz in the air; none knew what to expect. The justice slowly read Lilly's will: two and half million dollars to build a new city library and a small trust to help pay for local foster kids. The gymnasium fell quiet as an empty sepulcher. One by one—the older ones first—the townspeople hung their heads and departed in silent shame. Lilly was no longer silly. *Really.*

Bad Reaction

I once heard a story about two men walking down a city street. One stops to buy a paper from a local vendor. Upon paying and receiving the newspaper, the fellow said to the seller, "Thanks and good day!" The vendor replied, *"Oh, bugger off! What's good about it?"* The buying man then replied, "God bless you!" and then started again walking down the street. His companion turned to him and said, "Why were you so courteous to that nasty chap who was so rude to you? The buyer replied, "Because I act; *I don't react."*

We should take heed of this ditty, because so much of life is about dealing with nasty, difficult, and rude people. In many cases, some folk are just plain mean. We have a choice. We can fight fire with fire and be just as noxious and rude to people as they are to us, or we can take the high road. Being copasetic and friendly despite being treated otherwise is difficult. These days we seem to live in a world where everyone is looking out for number one, and no one cares who they offend or who they hurt. Ill-mannered behavior and gutter talk seem to be in vogue, and nice guys do seem to come in last. It seems like the meek will never inherit the earth.

But if we choose to live our lives by a higher standard that treats all people from all walks of life with respect—be them of high station or off the street—it is truly a credit to us and engenders our Maker proud. As He said, *"What you do for the least of these, you do for Me."*

It is not easy to be kind all the time, especially when been unkind to. Yet, He said, *"What credit it to you if you are only good to those who are good to you?"* If we are to be a shining light, we must do so at times that are not always at our choosing or personal preference. Being kind and civil at all times—acting, not reacting—takes a certain moral courage, and especially when done without some sense of duplicitous piety. It is simply living to a standard set from Above. This doesn't mean taking excessive crap from people or putting one's life in danger. Nor does it mean to be a mealy mouth milquetoast who is always sweet like a wimpy shrew. It simply means being able to take a stand for common decency and provision for fair treatment even if others do not reciprocate. *"Overcome evil with good,"* the scripture reads. It is the only way for a kinder, gentler world.

It is not being a martyr or any kind of heroism we are talking about; it is simply being as human as He was, which was amazing considering the pedigree of His deity.

My Popper

Celebrated journalist Tom Brokaw published a book *The Greatest Generation* (1998) in which he chronicles the life of many people of my grandfather's era. Like many in Brokaw's book, my grandfather whom we called Popper lived through the Great Depression and was a block warden in Detroit during the Second World War. Originally from a small farm in Prattville, Michigan, Popper was initially educated in a one room school house where reportedly he moved up three grades in one year. He went on to get his college degree and pursued career in teaching and higher education. With a doctorate in tow, he ended up president of a large university. As impressive as his professional career was, in fact what truly was remarkable was that he put all his younger seven siblings through college.

That wasn't the Popper I apperceived. Rather, growing up I knew him as strong, gentle, caring man who took me berry picking, fishing, golfing, and even whittling (carving wood). At our lake house he was all about chores from cutting trees and stacking wood to raking beaches. I was his gopher on many projects from building small habitations to fetching wildflowers for my aunt, mother and grandma whilst he patiently waited by the side of the road in his motorcar. I shagged balls for him on the golf course and was his wingman on many trips to town for home supplies or groceries.

Grandparents are great. They love you, are excited about you, and are proud of you for just being you. Lately, however, our "*greatest generation*" has become squeezed as they have so many new responsibilities. Many have to take care of their children's children as result of divorce or parental dislocation due to drugs or other family hardship. Many have to go back to work at an advanced age to support themselves or their offspring including their grandchildren. The "golden years" have become almost a misnomer as seniors are saddled with these burdensome responsibilities that previous generations had little to suffer. With many on fixed incomes combined with high medical costs, many seniors have to choose between putting food on the table or paying for needed prescription drugs. The age of seniors kicking back and savoring their later years seems to have gone the way of the dinosaur.

This new role in society for grandparents is just as indicative of the dissolution of the nuclear family in general. Television, tablets, iPhone and **PlayStations** have replaced backyard football or busy playgrounds in the local park. The young text each other at dinner rather than speak to each other and they no longer teach cursive writing in many schools. Parents are also caught up in the tech revolution spending dinner dates with iPhone on their table reading emails throughout the meal. Retinal eye contact has become facial recognition for computers and A.I. is paving the way for our" brave *new world."*

So where is God in all this? He is watching and cringing; He yearns for us to SLOW DOWN and have those quiet times where He is the main event, not the quick table blessing or an angry explicative so ubiquitously bandied about. Churches are merging due to lack of attendance, and many folk wearing the cloth have committed unspeakable, unsavory misdeeds. Truly a sad commentary.

Looking back, my Popper was a God-fearing man. He would not have liked the 21st century; and quite frankly, neither would it have probably liked him. *Regardless, I sure miss my Popper*

Ice Trays

It's a little peevish thing, but there is nothing more frustrating than when you get up in the morning, and you feel like an ice-cold soda. You go to the 'fridge and open the freezer section. You take out the ice cube trays and they are empty. *Somebody* didn't refill the ice trays (probably me).

The point is you *"reap what you sow"*—if you don't refill your ice cube trays, you have no ice. It is that simple. This aphorism is so true for many aspects of our lives. In our jobs, if we don't work enough hours, we can't pay our bills. In school, if we don't study enough, we don't do as well on our examinations. If we don't go to the store, we don't have as much food in the house. Without the bringing the right bait, we don't catch as many fish.

The same is true with health; this is something I know very well. I definitely mucked up in this area for which I have great regret. When younger I suffered some serious wrongs, and I dealt and coped with this by engaging in lots of food and drink; the result of this was I gained over two hundred pounds. In doing so, developed Adult Onset Type II diabetes. Thus, when I broke my ankle in 2015 and it became infected it would not heal. Massively strong antibiotics were used to save the leg (to no avail). Kidneys weak from the diabetes were now destroyed by the antibiotics. Now I have no leg and my kidneys are shot. As a result, I now on dialysis and am hoping for a kidney transplant. At the moment I am actively looking for a living donor.

I have no one to blame but myself. This lesson of *"reaping what you sow"* is also true in relationships. Any good friendship or marriage takes a lot of work, and if you take the time and effort to promote the relationship it will be a strong one. The same is true with our children. Probably the most important thing we can do as adults with our children is give them our time. The same also is true for our relationship with the Lord. We will get out of our relationship with the Lord what we put into it. He says, "*If you draw near to me, I will draw near to you.*" It isn't really a question of faith, but one of commitment. If your walk with God is only an hour on Sundays you will probably go through many dry seasons, just as if your friendship with a person is a phone call once a month. Good prayer life is important here, for it is one mainstay of a good relationship with the Maker. When in a good relationship with God, one wants to do good service work, whatever that might be; this is true for us for in our relationships even in small but important ways, like doing dishes or making sure there is food on the table for our children.

The bottom line is any relationship takes work. When we put time and energy into a friendship it will be strong, and there will be an impervious bond. As we nurture that bond we develop trust, which is the mainstay of any good relationship. And through obedience to Him, He learns to trust us even more, which also has many relational rewards like in any friendship. It feels good to be trusted, and He enjoys our trust as much as we relish His. With good trust we then become useful, which can give our lives purpose. In having purpose our lives have *meaning,* which is something I think we all want.

Many people who feel we live in a meaningless world do so by sowing anything but God. He is there if we just give Him a chance. *We just must try.*

Poopydoo

God hates grumblers and murmurers. This is made clear in the **Book of Numbers** where the Israelites became unhappy with their situation in the desert after the Lord had so miraculously delivered them from the Egyptian Pharaoh and his men by parting the Red Sea. As it says in Chapter 11:1:

"And the people grumbled and deplored their hardships, which was evil in ears of the Lord, and when the Lord heard it, His anger was kindled; and the fire of the Lord burned among them and devoured those in the outlying parts of the camp."

In **Psalm 95:** 10-11: *"Forty years long was I grieved and disgusted with that generation, and I said, it is a people who err in their hearts, and they do not approve or acknowledge, or regard My ways. Wherefore I swore in My wrath that they would never enter My rest."*

It is clear that the Lord does not appreciate those who are not grateful for His provision, whatever that might be. At times I have been guilty of this self-serving thanklessness. Even when I was in a good teaching position I would at times be unhappy with aspects of my job, or certain people or situations around me. Sometimes when things "hit the fan" or the going got tough, I could be found to murmur things like," *This really sucks*," or "*God hates me*," under my breath. The adult in me always knew I was blessed beyond measure, but the insolent child in me frequently found reasons to grouse and moan.

Fortunately, I have a wonderful wife who always has a handle on truth and sees the big picture. Even more recently when I got my leg amputated and my kidneys failed, if I started grumbling at God, she would sarcastically chide, "*Oh, so we have Mr. Poopydoo today"* Feeling a bit sorry for myself, she set me straight; she scolded, "*John David! You need to grow up and be thankful! You have a bad attitude. You have so many blessings!"* She would then list them all such as telling me to be grateful for having good insurance, and of one the best orthopedic surgeons in the State of Ohio. Furthermore, I have the blessings of a consistent means of income (disability), and a warm home and a loving wife. She would remind me that I have good friends, a loving family, and a supportive church, and on and on. Finally, I would give up the ghost and meekly apologize. She would shake her head at me and walk away with a slight air of plumb disgust or righteous indignation.

Always being grateful and thankful is the one keys to a fruitful and meaningful relationship with God. Even in bad or difficult situations, we can have a positive outlook. When Saint Paul was imprisoned in Rome, instead of grousing or complaining, he called himself an *"ambassador in chains,"* who could use his situation to still spread the gospel. He wrote in Philippians, *"Now I want you to know and continue to rest assured, brethren, that what [has happened] to me [this imprisonment] has actually only served to advance and give a renewed impetus to the [spreading of this] good news (the Gospel)."*

The bottom line is that regardless of the situation we are in we should be thankful. We do not always know why we are going through what we are suffering, but God does. He will no doubt always have some purpose to our pain. The trick is to see things through God's eyes (as my wife often does better than myself). Growing up, one of my father's favorite mantras was *"I choose to remain positive,"* no matter what the situation. They say *"attitude is everything,"* and we need the *"attitude of gratitude"* and they are all correct in saying so. On the other hand, in the same way God bemoans murmuring and grumbling, He finds favor with those who have are upbeat and positive attitude, even in bad situations. As one contemporary evangelist says, '*Your set back is only a set up for good things God has in store for you*' In the Old Testament Joseph was imprisoned thirteen years only to then be put second in command of all of Egypt allowing him to give food to his family in a time of famine. Daniel's rescue out of the Lion's Den ended up initiating a decree by King Darius that all in the land all his people should worship and *"tremble"* at the God of Daniel, *the Living God*. And, our Lord dying a rotten, stinking death on the cross was the essential linchpin ensuring our salvation.

So always take pains to have a good attitude. Don't be like me and be Poopydoo at times. It only serves to make Him irate. There is purpose to the pain. Even the beautiful Monarch butterfly has first to spend time as a lowly caterpillar taking a hiatus in a shoddy home-spun cocoon. *For this we too should take heed and learn.*

"Joekeeze!"

True story. When I was a lad about eight or nine years old I was riding in my best friend's station wagon going to the grocery. It was just me, my buddy, and his mother who was driving. We lived in a reasonably affluent suburban area, and it was a hot, humid, August day. As we were about halfway to the store, an old clunky dark colored *Malibu* adroitly pulled up beside us. There were two black men in the car. The driver of the car swung close next to us and yelled, *"Joekeeze!" "Joekeeze!"* Immediately my buddy's mom became frightened; she screamed at us, "Toby and Jack, roll your windows up and lock your doors! Look straight ahead! *Do not look at them or say a word!"* She hit the gas. Yet, the *Malibu* still kept pace and the black man on the driver side kept yelling, *"Joekeeze! Joekeeze!!"* My friend's mother sped off and eventually left them in the dust.

When we got to the grocery store my friend's mother was visibly shaken, and pale as a ghost. When she gathered herself, we went into the store and did our shopping. When we finished a bag, boy carried her groceries to the car. My friend's mother gave the car keys to the bag boy and politely said, "Put 'em in the back." The bag boy reached out to unlock the back of the station wagon only to blurt, "But lady, your keys are already in the lock." All of us stared at the back of the station wagon. Her spare keys were hanging off the back of the car. All the sudden it sunk in. The African American fellow was just trying to do us a huge favor calling attention to the keys. I looked over at my friend's mother who held her head down in deep shame. I also felt regret.

An important lesson I leaned that day. One I have never forgotten.

Big C

My dear friend Michael has cancer, as does two other close comrades. It's breaking my heart, for I feel so helpless to stand by and watch. Yeah. I stand by and toss my little prayers heavenward, only to hear of more trips to radiation and another round of chemo. In both cases, these "cures" are almost worse than the cause. Treatment after treatment, only to find their numbers are worsening. Every cell of my body wants to scream bloody murder and shake my fist at the Big Guy.

Cancer is a strange animal to say the least: good cells gone crazy. Free radicals that decided to completely misbehave. Truth be known, we all have cancer cells in each of us. For most of us they are limited and lie dormant. For others the onslaught has begun, and the timeclock is ticking. For those afflicted nothing is more frightening, especially if they are children.

I am lucky. I am on dialysis, and I might be able to last another ten years maybe more. But I still have a limited time capsule, and I do see the finish line clearly. Like those with cancer, I want to cry "foul" and wonder why me? I pray that query and never seem really get an answer.

We all have a limited time on this rotating big blue ball. What we do with our lives is up to us. Some go for big coin, whilst others go soft touch with high reward. Regardless, we all make the best go of what we can, and hope that in the end, we might find peace and a place in the stars.

As I write I peer out my window. It is a frosty winter morn. Snow is on the ground. The sun is just rising over my neighbor's roof, and bright rays are spilling into my kitchen; I can see the dust particles dancing and prancing in the bright light. I can hear the java percolating in our old-style coffee maker; the aroma spills throughout the room. I look down at my left wrist and see the tiny puncture wounds from dialysis yesterday. My mind again returns to Michael and others whose lives I want to help but have no control. I pray and place them in His hands for I know that ultimately, He is in charge. I must let go. Resignation of control of the future gives inward appreciation of the present—for all of us.

I go to church, put coin in the plate, and try to be a do-gooder. With feigned hubris I would like to think I know where I am going when the last card is played. In some ways, my destination is out of my hands, and that is a bit unsettling regardless of my devoted faith and continual quest for His favor. I can only hope for the warm tunnel of light come splash-down—that and His strong arms wrapped firmly around me.

In the end we are all in this together. Humanity is something we all rent and never own. Let us all share this trip with love, smell the roses along the way, and always no matter what— be thankful.

Lost Doves

Here is a short narrative I heard in a sermon a long time ago; this is my version:

It was Christmas Eve. The man sipped his coffee whilst his family bundled up to go outside in the winter cold; they were leaving to go to the Christmas Eve service at the local church just a few miles down the country road. Their car was parked just outside the barn. The man chose not to go with them. It wasn't that he was against religion in general; it was just that he couldn't get wrap his mind around this whole God becoming man thing—*it just didn't make sense.*

It was bitter cold and there was deep snow. The capricious wind was fierce as the family trudged out of the farmhouse to their car. The man watched from the side door to make sure they got off alright. After they left, he returned to the kitchen and sat down to imbibe in more java. After a few moments he heard a huge gust of wind slam against the farmhouse. As the kitchen windows shuddered greatly, he then heard a large crashing sound out by the tool shed. He went to the window to see, but the thick snow coming down obscured his view. He threw on his hat, gloves, and jacket. He took his flashlight and went outside in the swirling winter storm. The tool shed was next to the barn, which was about fifty yards from the farmhouse. It was rough going in the snow, but the man finally made it to the large tool shed. To his chagrin, the wind had ripped the door of the shed off, and snow was drifting inside. As he tried to put the pieces of the broken door back on its hinges, he heard a noise. He looked down and spied five white doves lying in the ground in the midst of the snow and broken glass and wood from the remains of the busted shed door. *"Hmmm. They must have come in to get out of this weather,"* he surmised. He watched them for a moment; they were seemed totally lost and confused, clucking and cooing whilst the stormy winter wind blew them about on the shed floor. As the man watched he felt a pang of compassion for the little lost birds. He had to figure a way to get them to safety. He then reasoned, *"If I could only get them in the barn a few yards away they would be warm and dry.*" So he tried to pick them up, one by one but to no avail. He arduously tried to usher them out of the shed to guide them into the barn, but they scattered. He took off his coat and tried to scoop them up by laying his coat over them, but they were too quick. The man frantically looked about. The wind was now worse than ever, and the snow was drifting in the shed by the minute. The situation was getting desperate. He had to find some way of getting these lost doves into the barn while there was still time before the storm got worse. Almost at wits end, a random thought struck him: *"If I were just a dove for one minute, I could lead them into the barn myself and they would follow me!"* In that moment, all of the sudden he had a revelation; it hit him like a ton of bricks. He knew why God had become man. God had to become one of us humans like the doves to lead us into the barn (heaven) Himself—to get us warm and dry, so to speak; to corral us for all eternity. At that point he knew he couldn't help the doves anymore this evening, so he placed a large tarp over the shed's doorway and nailed it down securely; it was the best he could do. Maybe he could help them later when the storm was over if they were still alive. As he plodded his way back to the farmhouse there was almost a new skip in his step. His heart was warm, and he was excited beyond measure. He finally knew why God became man— what an epiphany! He couldn't wait to tell his wife when she returned. Later, when she and the kids pulled up and made it into the house, he grabbed her and gave her a big hug. "*Merry Christmas!*" he emphatically exclaimed. She looked at him kind of oddly, and said, "What has gotten into you, Honey?" He just smiled, and said, "Nothing dear. I just figured something out. Let's talk about it over some hot chocolate with the kids." She nodded and they all got together and had a great discussion about what Dad had discovered that night regarding the lost doves, the barn, God, and man.

--a simple, hopeful story, but a good one nonetheless

Epilogue

We choose our own path for work. Mine was teaching. Now stuck in this house recovering from ten major surgeries I have spent over three years in relative solitude save for my wife and two dogs. This has been a far cry from the classroom full of the vibrancy and joy that comes from the intellectual banter and daily relational satisfaction that occurs between teacher and student.

All this, I miss very much. Now I have a different calling. As mentioned before: Saint Paul's calling during his time in a Roman prison was to pen the epistles of the New Testament. I don't write epistles; rather, I do my best to manage to write meaningful ditties and spiritual reflections.

Is my 40 months of house arrest meant for good? I do not know. I have grown closer and more tenderhearted toward my wife and have a much deeper relationship with the Lord through my protracted ordeal. Further, I have written two books which hitherto I had not time nor the inclination to write. I have a much greater appreciation for those who suffer, and for those who are not ambulatory. And I have become much more proficient at music and guitar, as I have had bountiful time to practice and compose.

Moreover, I asked the Lord to heal me—to remove from me my maladies (leg and kidney), yet instead I often just sensed the Lord saying, *"My power is made perfect in weakness."* So I began to ponder the true meaning of my ordeal, coming to the conclusion that with this extended time it wasn't just for me to write, or produce faith-based poetry. It wasn't just to humble me and make me a better person. It wasn't necessarily punishment for prior wrongdoing on my part. Rather, it was simply to put me a position where He could be my one and only joy, save for my wife, dogs, and endless channel surfing. God is a jealous God, and He wants to be numero uno. In all my years of teaching, I attended church, tinkered with faith-based poetry, and did typical service work. Yet, in many ways I was far from Him. So, like the shepherds who would break the legs of a young wayward sheep to teach them obedience, God broke mine. In those day the shepherds would then place the young lamb over the shepherd's shoulders and carrying them until healing was complete; this would then make the lamb totally dependent upon the shepherd. Once the lamb was healed it would never leave the shepherd again. Now through this adversity, I guess I am a bit like the lost and broken legged sheep. Now I know that He truly is mine, and I think more importantly—He knows that I am forever His. For this I am eternally grateful.

In the **Book of Romans,** it says *"All things work for good for those who love God and called according to His purpose."* In some ways, losing my leg, and ending up on dialysis seems a far cry from "good." Yet, one has to realize that the scripture does not read that all things work for MY good—only that they work for good, the implication being that it may be for His overall good. Having said this, I have come to realize that my travail—my suffering may just be part of His overall plan of the like of which I may never understand nor comprehend in the least. And that is okay. I would much rather He call the shots, even if I end up down here on the short end of the stick. If He wants me to *"take one for the team,"* so be it. Sometimes in life we just have to shut ones mouth and lump it.

So I walk away—with a prosthesis, mind you, with the greater knowledge and illumination of Who and What He is. And like the quarterback who was benched, but still gets the championship ring, I am thankfully now a substitute player. I can't work, or do many things I did before, but am truly grateful and thankful in spite of my infirmities. And come to think of it, isn't that what it is about after all? Giving Him the unconditional love He shows me? That, in the end was the greatest lesson of all. *And for this spiritual instruction, I am most grateful indeed! Amen.*

About the Book and its Author

J.D. Emens received his undergraduate degree from Kenyon College where he was a four-year All-American athlete. He received his Master's degree from the London school of Economics, and his Doctorate from Miami University. He also attended seminary at The Methodist Theological School in Ohio. He taught at the college level for twenty-five years, most of which was at The Ohio State University on the Marion Campus; during his tenure there he was twice voted "*Teacher of the Year*" by the student body. In the fall of 2015, he fell and shattered his ankle. His diabetic leg became infected, and after ten surgeries over a three-year period the leg was eventually amputated. During this time strong antibiotics were used to try and save the leg, and their liberal use further compromised his kidneys. Emens is now in complete kidney failure and is now on dialysis hoping to have a transplant.

"*Always More French Fries at the Bottom of the Bag,*" is a collection of poems and spiritual reflections that intuits a broken man embracing his stark and challenging circumstances though the written word. As the title of the book suggests, Emens is clearly an optimist, and strongly believes that through devoted faith, joy and peace can prevail despite tragedy. No matter how bad or onerous a situation, Emens feels good can come from it. His struggle has only strengthened his conviction and drawn him closer to his Maker. His poetry and reflections mirror his deepened spiritual walk, and this indeed is what he ardently wishes to convey and share through the written word.

He is the author of "*Boom! & Adversity*" (2018), and the text, "*WTO Panel Dynamics*" (2007/12). He lives with his wife and two dogs in Marion, Ohio. He has two children and two grandchildren.

Made in the USA
Columbia, SC
13 September 2022

67144817R00050